THE SEQUOIA LIVES ON

THE SEQUOIA LIVES ON

JOANNA COOKE

ILLUSTRATED BY
FIONA HSIEH

Yosemite Conservancy
YOSEMITE NATIONAL PARK

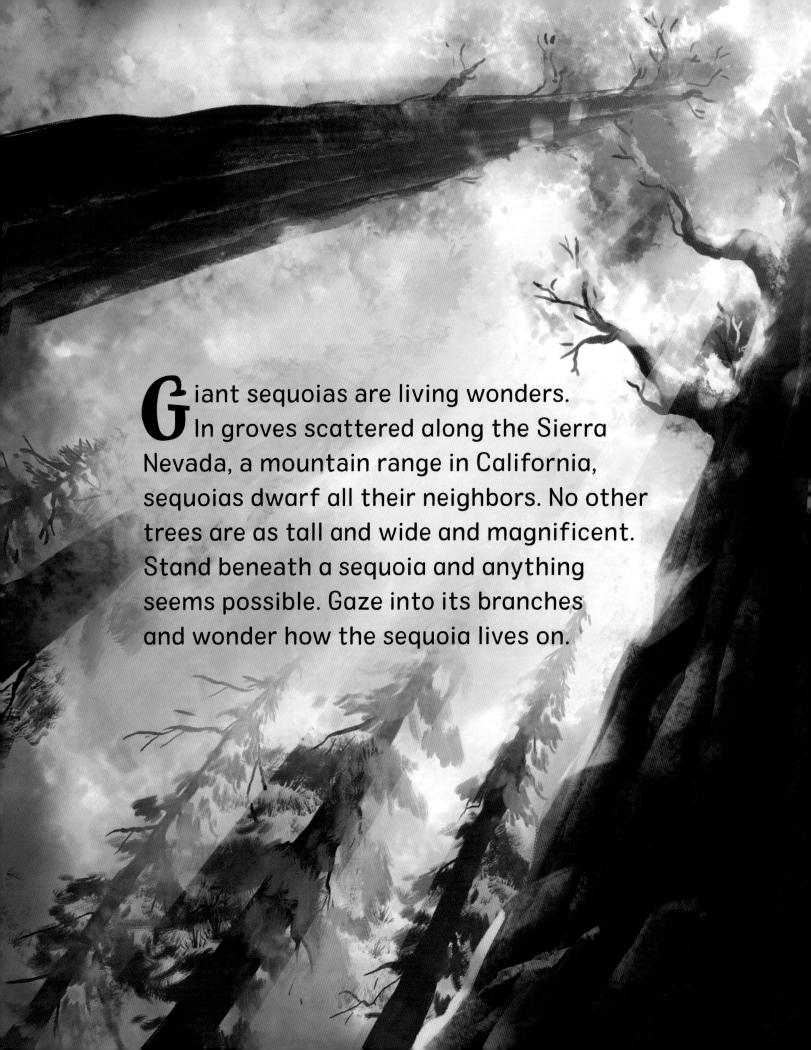

Giant sequoias are living wonders. In groves scattered along the Sierra Nevada, a mountain range in California, sequoias dwarf all their neighbors. No other trees are as tall and wide and magnificent. Stand beneath a sequoia and anything seems possible. Gaze into its branches and wonder how the sequoia lives on.

The sequoia is Earth's most massive tree, the height of three blue whales stacked chin to tail and weighing even more. It begins life as most trees do—as a seed, a flake no bigger than an ant.

How does such a tiny seed grow into a tree as heavy as three hundred elephants?

The sequoia seed relies on fire. A blaze crawls on the forest floor, clearing away fallen leaves and broken branches in which a seed might disappear. Rising heat from the fire warms the sequoia's scaly cones, drying and opening them, then setting the brown seeds adrift in smoke-filled air, floating toward a place to grow.

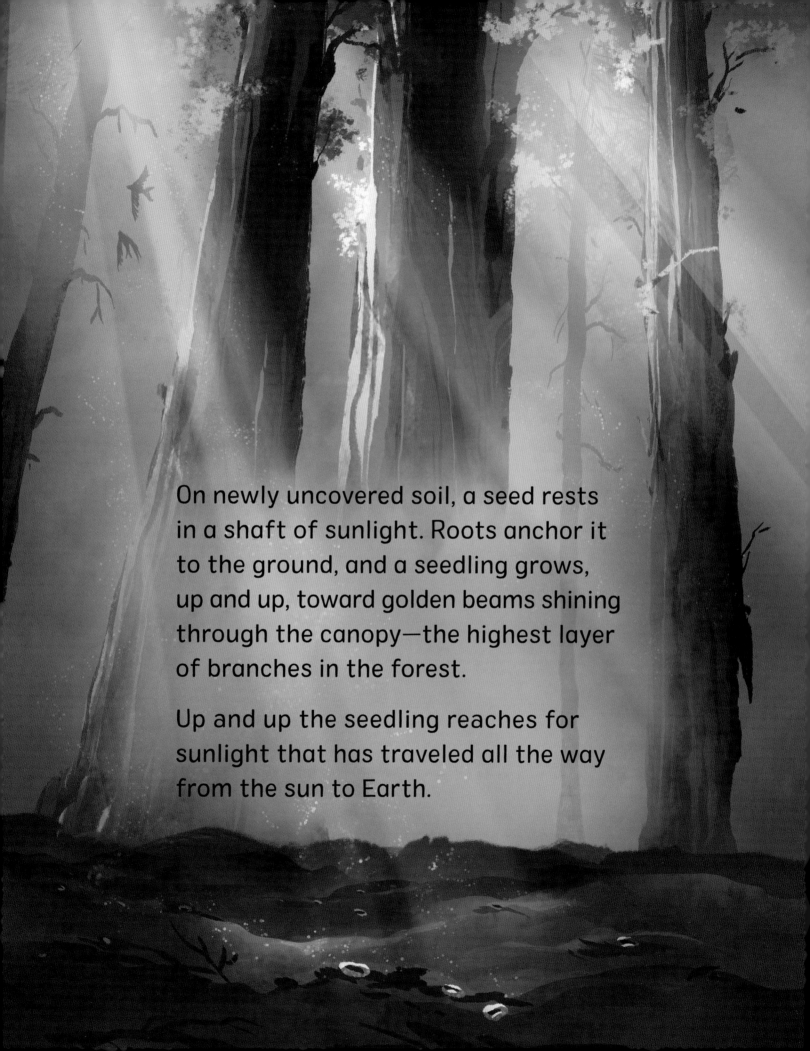

On newly uncovered soil, a seed rests in a shaft of sunlight. Roots anchor it to the ground, and a seedling grows, up and up, toward golden beams shining through the canopy—the highest layer of branches in the forest.

Up and up the seedling reaches for sunlight that has traveled all the way from the sun to Earth.

Sequoia leaves take in that sunlight
and also air. Exhale and your breath
could become food for a sequoia.

And the sequoia lives on.

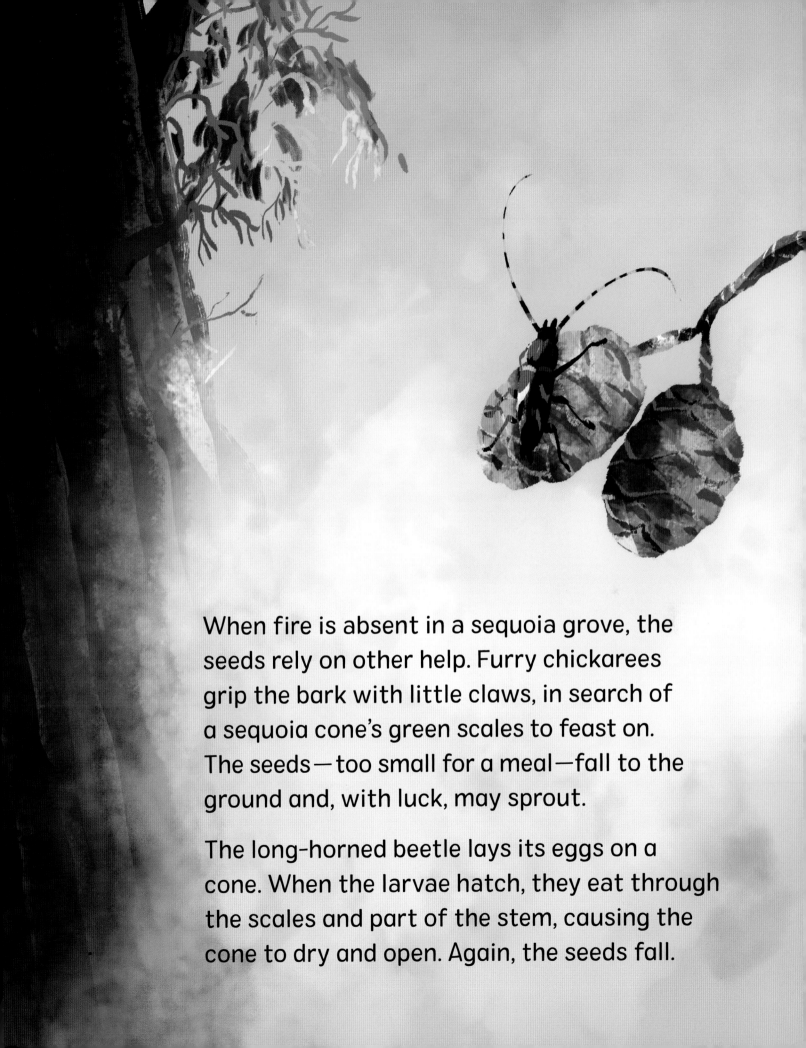

When fire is absent in a sequoia grove, the seeds rely on other help. Furry chickarees grip the bark with little claws, in search of a sequoia cone's green scales to feast on. The seeds—too small for a meal—fall to the ground and, with luck, may sprout.

The long-horned beetle lays its eggs on a cone. When the larvae hatch, they eat through the scales and part of the stem, causing the cone to dry and open. Again, the seeds fall.

Buried in the earth, a sequoia's roots reach outward, creating a hidden foundation as wide as the tree is tall.

Each day, a large sequoia's roots absorb enough water to fill more than eight bathtubs.

From across the forest, a sequoia's colorful bark almost glows. Thicker at the tree's base than at the top, the spongy bark swells into buttresses that support the sequoia's growing bulk.

How long will it take for a new sequoia seedling
to become so big? Humans can live more than
eighty years—a mere blink in the life of a sequoia.
After two human lifetimes, a sequoia will have
grown old enough to make cones.

With enough sunlight, air, and water, a mighty
sequoia can live more than thirty human lifetimes.
Imagine a sequoia so old and so huge not even a
ring of twenty children holding hands could hug it.

Giants among giants.

Some are even grander.

An old sequoia's trunk may be hollowed out by fire. Its crown, once pointed like a pyramid, is now a snag-top, broken by lightning and wind.

Lower branches grow upward, filling openings in the canopy. The expanded crown holds more leaves, which means more food for growing. Even black and scarred, an old sequoia can produce a gallon of tiny seeds—more than 300,000—each year.

And the sequoia lives on.

Over time, such immensity can harm an ancient sequoia. Season after season, its branches thicken and grow heavy. Broader than nearby pines and cedars, the great branches overwhelm the damaged trunk and shallow roots, and the sequoia falls.

Shaking the ground upon impact, the tree shatters into car-sized blocks and toothpick-tiny pieces.

And still the sequoia lives on.

Stretched across the forest floor,
the fallen sequoia decomposes over
hundreds of years. The massive trunk
now rests side by side with new seedlings
reaching for golden beams of light.

The cycle of the giants begins again,
with one tiny seed.

WONDERFUL SEQUOIAS

WHERE GIANT SEQUOIAS LIVE

Giant sequoias, *Sequoiadendron giganteum*, are rare. Fossil records show that the trees ranged across North America, Europe, and Asia over a hundred million years ago, when dinosaurs still roamed the earth. Today, sequoias are native to only about seventy groves, or groups of trees, spread across the Sierra Nevada of California. The western slopes of these mountains provide the wet, mild winters and dry, warm summers necessary for sequoia survival.

GIANT SEQUOIAS REALLY ARE GIANT

Giant sequoias hold the record for volume—they take up more space than any other tree with a single trunk. A tree named the General Sherman, located in Sequoia National Park, is the biggest, measuring 52,508 cubic feet (1,487 cubic meters). And that's just the trunk! By comparison, the volume of the record-holding blue whale—the largest animal to ever live—is only about 5,000 cubic feet (142 cubic meters). The average blue whale measures 80 to 100 feet (24 to 30 meters), while sequoias can reach 270 feet (82 meters) or more in height! But they are not the tallest trees. That distinction belongs to the sequoia's close relative, the coast redwood.

SEEDS ON THE MOVE

Sequoia cones are "serotinous." This means that a disturbance triggers their opening. For sequoias, that trigger is often fire, which creates the best conditions for seeds to sprout. A natural part of Sierra Nevada ecosystems, low-intensity fire converts the nutrients found in dead plant material into a form more usable by living plants. Also, as warm air from the fire rises, it dries the sequoia cones and releases the seeds to the forest floor. The chickaree (also known as the Douglas squirrel) and the long-horned wood-boring beetle's larvae also help disperse sequoia seeds. While neither animal prepares the soil for seed growth as fire does, they do help get more seeds to the ground, which means a greater chance for new sequoias to sprout.

WHAT DO SEQUOIAS EAT?

Sequoias have millions or sometimes billions of miniature overlapping leaves with which to absorb sunlight and carbon dioxide, a gas that is in the air we breathe. Inside each leaf, green chlorophyll combines that sunlight and carbon dioxide with water brought up from the roots to make a simple sugar trees use to grow and make cones and seeds.

SEQUOIA BARK

A sequoia's bark is thickest near the tree's base and ranges from 6 to 36 inches (15 to 91 centimeters) thick. That's as thick as five new pencils lined up end to end are long! The bark's famous red-orange color comes from a natural substance called tannin that helps protect the trees from insects, disease, and fire.

GIANT SEQUOIA LIFESPAN

Ancient sequoias can live between 1,500 and 2,500 years, or about as long as thirty human lifetimes. Current science suggests that the oldest known sequoia lived an estimated 3,200 years, which is like living approximately forty human lifetimes! Still, sequoias are younger than the bristlecone pines, also found in California. The oldest known bristlecone is more than 5,000 years old. Fallen sequoias help support a healthy forest by returning their nutrients to the soil as they break down, or decompose. As other plants and fungi in the grove absorb those nutrients, the sequoia's energy can be said to live on.

PROTECTING GIANT SEQUOIAS

Most sequoia groves are protected in state and national parks, forests, and monuments. Current challenges to sequoia survival include changes in Earth's climate, a long history of natural fire suppression, and other human impacts. Basing their actions on scientific discoveries, park leaders and conservation groups are working to protect shallow root systems from exposure and soil compaction, to support the natural flow of water, and to safely reintroduce fire into groves. New science (including information about how giant sequoias respond to dry periods such as California's warm drought of 2011–2016) helps us make informed choices to protect giant sequoias.

CONTINUED...

VISITING A SEQUOIA GROVE

You can protect giant sequoias too. When visiting a sequoia grove, practice these Leave No Trace principles:

- Respect trail signs and closed areas.
- Leave sequoia cones and seeds on the ground.
- Take all trash—even picnic crumbs!—with you.

Your family or school class can also help by joining a conservation group or volunteering. Most importantly, learn all you can about our living planet. The future of giant sequoias will depend on young people like you continuing to care for these amazing trees.

Text copyright © 2018 by Joanna Cooke
Illustrations copyright © 2018 by Fiona Hsieh

Published in the United States by Yosemite Conservancy.
All rights reserved.

No portion of this work may be reproduced or transmitted in any form without the written permission of the publisher, except in the case of brief quotations embodied in critical articles or reviews.

Library of Congress Control Number: 2017956269

Design by Katie Jennings Campbell

ISBN 978-1-930238-85-5

Printed in China

4 5 6 – 22

FOR LUPIN,
WHO STARTED
IT ALL –J.C.

Yosemite Conservancy inspires people to support projects and programs that preserve Yosemite and enrich the visitor experience.

YOSEMITE
CONSERVANCY®

yosemite.org